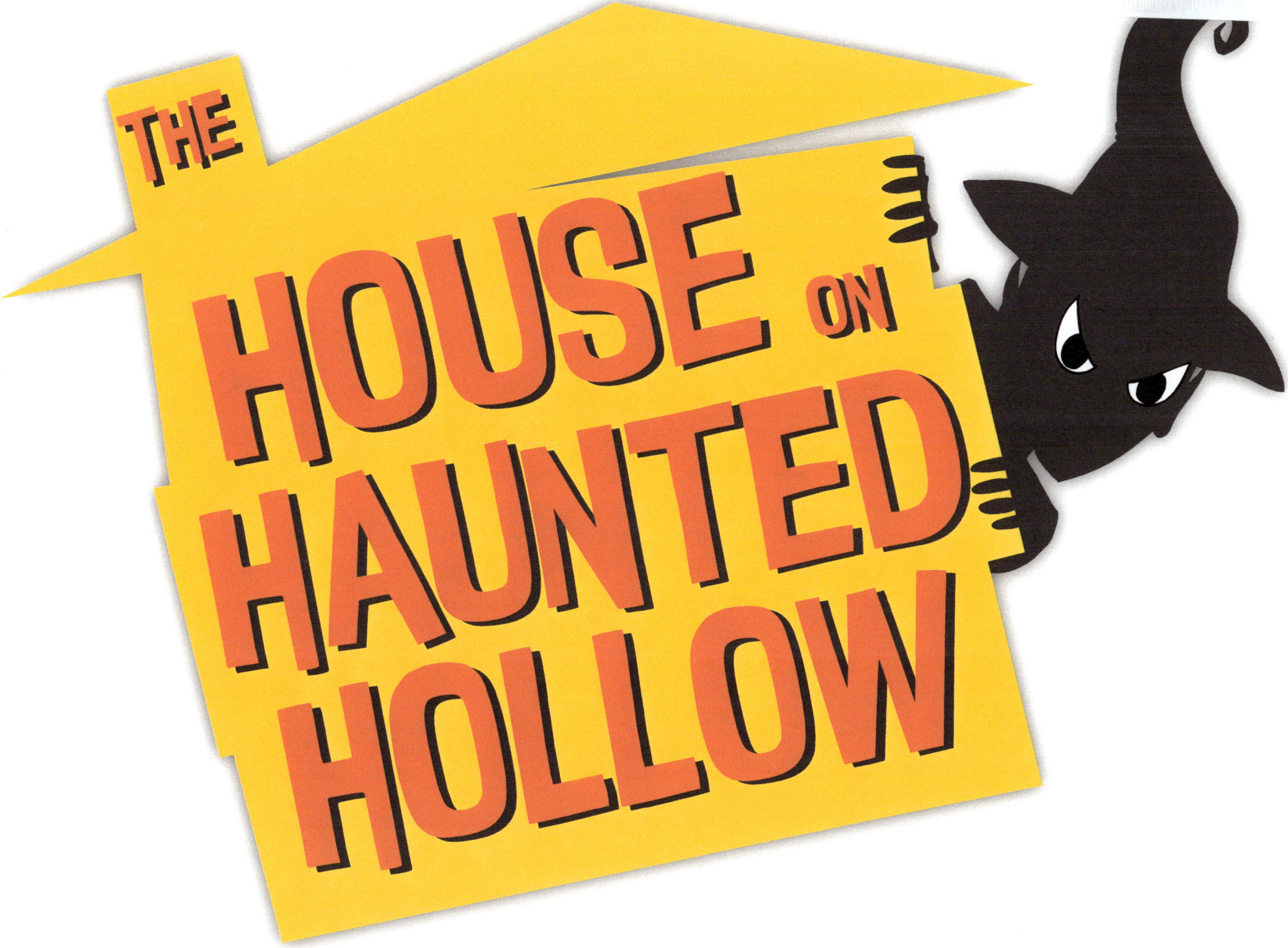

THE HOUSE ON HAUNTED HOLLOW

THE HOUSE ON HAUNTED HOLLOW
by Christopher R. Fox and Dayton Young

Writer: Dayton Young
Illustrator: Christopher R. Fox

Special thanks to all that have helped us acheive this goal and dream of ours.

The House on Haunted Hollow is copyright © 2019 by Mr. Fox and Mr. Owl, Christopher R. Fox and Dayton Young. All rights reserved. No part of this publication may be reproduced, stored in a retrieval system or transmitted, in any form or by any means, electronic, mechanical, photocopying, recorded or otherwise, without the prior permission of the copyright holders. Permission to duplicate materials from *The House on Haunted Hollow* must be obtained from Christopher R. Fox and Dayton Young. Permission to quote or reproduce for reviews and notices must be obtained from the respective copyright holders. *The House on Haunted Hollow* website may be accessed at www.mrfoxstudios.com

ISBN 978-0-9909275-3-2   Second Edition: February 2019   Made in USA

This is a story of fear and fright
that happened one spooky Halloween night.

Every word is true, although it may be hard to swallow the tale of *The House on Haunted Hollow* ...

Four friends had gathered to go trick-or-treating
and were dreaming of the sweets that they'd soon be eating:

chocolate bars, lollipops, caramels and bon bons!
But first, they had to put their costumes on.

Chris was a spaceman, ready to explore.
Jason was a baseball player, hoping to score.

Zoey was a dragon who loves to fly
and breathe fire as she flies across the sky.

Daniel was a superhero with his side-kick handy,
and they all couldn't wait to get their hands on lots of candy!

Their parents took pictures and said "Smile and say cheese!
And don't forget to say 'Thank you!' And don't forget to say 'Please!'

Have fun with the goblins and ghosts and ghouls.
But remember this one, important rule:

stay away from the house on Haunted Hollow.
If other children go, please do not follow to the house on Haunted Hollow."

So off the friends went into the night,
carrying their candy bags and – of course – a flashlight.

They knocked on every neighbor's door;
they knocked and knocked and knocked some more.

They smiled and shouted "Trick or treat!
Give me something good to eat!"

They filled their bags up to the top.
They filled them up until it was time to stop.

"Come on, let's go back home," said Chris.
"So we can start eating all of this."

But on their way back, they passed by a door that they didn't remember passing before.

The windows were broken and the roof had a droop,
and there was a Jack-O-Lantern sitting right there on the stoop.

All in all it was a frightful sight.
Zoey said, "Let's have one more trick-or-treat tonight."

"That house looks too scary," said Jason with a chill.
"If you won't go up there," said Chris, "I will."

"Yeah, don't be a chicken," said Zoey. "We'll be fine."
But then Daniel read the words on the nearest street sign.

"Haunted Hollow. Oh, no! Oh, no!
I agree with Jason ... I don't think we should go."

"Stop acting like a wimp," said Chris with a grin.
"We're just going to knock. We aren't going to go in."

"We'll be quick," said Zoey. "Don't worry, you'll see. Now quit whining, fall in line and follow me."

Zoey went first, then Jason, Chris and Daniel,
and finally Daniel's not-so-heroic Cocker Spaniel.

They opened the front gate and made their way down the path. Jason said, "This is worse than taking a bath!"

Daniel was so scared he could hardly peek.
As they climbed on the porch, they could hear it groan and creak.

They got close enough to knock on the door ...
but the old porch was broken and they fell through the floor!

When the dust finally settled, their hearts filled with fear as they saw horrible, awful, monsters were near!

A vampire, a werewolf, a slime and a slug,
an alien, a goblin, and a big, ugly bug!

Zoey started screaming and Chris let out a shout.
"We're sorry we came in! We just want to get out!"

They ran to this corner and they ran over there.
They ran in that direction ... they ran everywhere!

Every window was closed and every doorknob was locked.
Yes, every possible way to get out was blocked.

Jason began panicking while Daniel hid behind his cape.
His side-kick just whimpered, because there was no escape.

The monsters surrounded the four terrified friends who huddled together and wondered, "Is this the end?"

They shut their eyes tight – yes, even the pup –
and hoped the monsters wouldn't be there when they opened their eyes up.

The darkness grew darker and the coldness grew colder ... when suddenly Chris felt a hand on his shoulder.

"Oh please, get away and leave us alone.
My friends and I just want to go home!"

But the four friends opened their eyes and found that there weren't any monsters around!

Instead of scary creatures, they saw mom and dad, and boy, oh boy, were the children glad!

They told their parents the story from the beginning and their parents just listened, nodding and grinning.

"Quit making up stories and get ready for bed.
You have school tomorrow," their parents said.

So the children all waved and said "Good-bye!"
and went home happy just to be alive.

Outside there was lightning and rain and thunder which made it a perfectly gloomy time to wonder,

were the monsters not as bad as they seemed?
Or was it all just some terrible dream?